HEY, KIDDO

by Jarrett J. Krosoczka

graphix

An Imprint of

SCHOLASTIC

Library of Congress Control Number Available

ISBN 978-0-545-90247-2 (hardcover)
ISBN 978-0-545-90248-9 (paperback)

10 9 8 7 6 5 4 3 2 1   18 19 20 21 22

Printed in China   62
First edition, October 2018
Edited by David Levithan
Color and lettering by Jarrett J. Krosoczka
Book design by Phil Falco
Creative Director: David Saylor

For Joe and Shirl

For Leslie

For every reader who recognizes
this experience. I see you.

JJK

PROLOGUE

CITY OF WORCESTER

Hope Cemetery

Established 1854

Won't need to worry about getting a ride from anyone.

Grandpa has trouble seeing at night with all of the headlights coming at him, so he's never able to drive me anywhere.

Grandma only drives when she absolutely has to. So, like, doctors' appointments and that sort of stuff.

Other than that, she only ever drives down the street to Iandoli's for groceries.

Lynn and Holly used to drive me around whenever they could, but they're so busy with their own families now.

I don't want to bother them.

My grandfather loves his parents. Really loves them. He always makes sure we stop and say a prayer for them whenever we are here.

There are a lot of empty plots at the bottom of the hill. Maybe that's where I will go someday. It would only make sense for me to end up near them—they raised me, after all. And my mother? Who knows where she'll end up. Honestly, it's surprising that she isn't here already. And my father? Who knows if I'll ever even meet the guy before either of us make it to the grave.

C'mon. Let's get going.

HENNESSY'S

(The Rock)

GLAD YOU DROPPED IN

Mr. and Mrs. Clarence Olson
request the honor of your presence
at a Dinner and Wedding Reception
for their daughter

Shirley Ruth
and
Joseph D. Krosoczka
son of
Mr. and Mrs. Joseph Krosoczka
Saturday afternoon, August twenty-eight
nineteen hundred and forty-eight
at one o'clock
P. N. A. Hall, 49 Lafayette Street
Worcester, Massachusetts

To "Joe"
May the future
hold for us as
happiness as in
in the past.
Love,
"Shirl"
'48

CHAPTER 1
FAMILY HISTORY

Shirley, my grandmother, was in study hall when Joe, my grandfather, walked in for the first time. As Shirley always told the story, she stopped on a dime at the sight of him.

Who is that? That is the man for me.

15

There was a full moon on their first date.

And that was their first kiss. I imagine that Joe was only able to keep up his ruse for so long, because eventually Shirley would graduate in the spring of 1945 and he wouldn't.

But Joe had something bigger on his mind than graduating.

'44

He wanted to see the world and serve his country during WWII.

He wasn't seventeen yet, so he got creative with his birth date on his enrollment papers.

Which is why he accepted the misspelling of Krasoczki, his last name, on his papers.

Joe helped build the highways in Guam, and while he was away, he received a breakup letter from Shirley. He was devastated. But he also seemed to enjoy his time in Guam...

I don't know how, but when Joe returned, he won back Shirley's heart and they were married.

It was a controversial union—Joe's parents were Catholics who'd immigrated to the U.S. from Poland, while Shirley's parents were Protestants who'd immigrated from Sweden.

When they settled into life together, Joe needed money. So he took work wherever he could get it.

When he saw a bunch of neckties on sale at a department store downtown, he saw a golden opportunity.

NECKTIES
Sale 5¢

Joe made a killing that first day. So he went back out day after day.

One afternoon, he had some extra money in his back pocket, so he treated himself to a coffee and a piece of pie at a local diner.

Good afternoon, officer.

Sir.

How goes the beat today?

Well, there's this guy going door to door selling ties without a license.

We've been getting lots of complaints. You haven't seen anything, have ya?

Nope.

Well, good luck to ya! I hope that you find the guy.

That was the last day Joe sold ties.

Joe and Shirl started having children, and Joe was cooking up a plan to make some money to support his new family.

First came Joey.

And then Leslie, my mother.

In that same year, 1955, Joe opened up a factory to produce piping for sinks.

While he worked day and night, more kids came into the picture. Stephen arrived.

And then, with three kids in tow,
Shirley had a miscarriage.

It threw her.

Shirley eventually got pregnant again and wanted to name the baby Holly; she'd always loved that name. But the lady who lived across the street had a cat named Holly.

Holly! Come here, Holly! Oh, where is that damn cat?

So they named that baby Lynn.

Shirley found herself pregnant yet again within a few months of Lynn's birth. And during that pregnancy, the neighbor's cat died.

She and Joe named their fifth kid Holly.

And how did my parents meet? How did I come into this world? I don't know many of the details of it. I just know that it was at my father's family's bar. He was onstage, playing with his band.

I always imagined my mother caught his eye while he strummed his guitar.

However they found each other, they did, and they managed to hide it from my father's girlfriend. And then my mother got pregnant...

My father backed off, claiming that the baby wasn't his. Supposedly, his girlfriend started spreading stories about how my mother had been sleeping around, so the baby could have belonged to anybody.

And sure, she had been sleeping around, but my mom knew he was the father as soon as I was born—I was white. All of her other boyfriends hadn't been.

I came home in an oversized stocking on Christmas Day.

BABY'S HEALTH RECORD

'S NAME Jarrett Joseph Krosoczka

Dr. Passey
mon.-Thurs. Fri.

VISITING THE DOCTOR ALWAYS TAKE THIS BOOK

CHAPTER 2
LIFE WITH LESLIE

When my mother had me, she was still living at home. My grandfather bought her a house on Bauer Street for her to raise me in. We had a nice little life there for a few years...

Even though we

ain't got money ...

I have random memories of my time living there with my mom. I remember my Big Bird doll and the Sesame Street pictures on the wall next to my crib. I remember my Charlie Brown, Snoopy, and Lucy bath toys and the feel of the smooth plastic when it was wet.

I remember eating Franken Berry cereal and saving all of the marshmallows for the final scoops. I remember my mom dressing me up for Halloween or for New Year's and then putting me up on the countertop to take photos.

I also remember strangers coming in and out of the house.

I had this recurring dream when I was a kid. I was in the middle of a field. And there were these monsters surrounding me on all sides, creeping in from the woods.

But if I looked at them, stared them right down, they'd freeze. The only problem was that every time I froze a monster with my eye contact, another monster would creep up behind me.

So I'd spin around and stare that one down. The monsters would inevitably creep closer and closer. I would spin around faster and faster, trying to stop them all, but eventually they'd loom over me.

I told you not to come barging in here! You stay in your room! Get back to your room!

At Christmastime, Mom and I went to the Auburn Mall.
I loved being so little that I could hide in the clothes racks.

Check out these scarves.
Lynn and Holly would love
these scarves, right?

DING DONG

My mother and I made some good memories there on Bauer Street.

But as Joe expected, she was making some terrible decisions.

CLICK

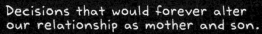

Decisions that would forever alter our relationship as mother and son.

I wouldn't see my mother for a long while after that day. Lynn and Holly would later tell me that after they babysat me over on Bauer Street, they would come home in tears, telling Joe and Shirl that they needed to do something. They needed to get me out of that house.

And when I slept over at my grandparents' house one night, I remarked at how amazed I was that they served me breakfast in the morning. As a three-year-old, I was getting my cereal on my own, because I was waking up in an empty house.

Determined to keep me, Joe convinced Leslie to sign the paperwork relinquishing parental rights. Joe became my legal guardian. The only way Leslie would sign the agreement was if Shirley wasn't a part of it. Leslie knew Joe would take care of me, but she didn't trust her mother. Not with their fiercely argumentative history.

I didn't know any of this. I just knew I had a new home.

GATES
LANE
GATORS
SCHOOL

Spectrum House
presents
Christmas 1982

De...
...
Recie...
feelin...
else...

that...
sinc...
you...
few...
way...
thin...
pret...
so...
now...
ber...
that...
from...
a lo...
you...
one...
don...
war...
in...
with...
be there yet.

a teleph...
why i dd...
very, very...
that you...
you more...
any where.

How is...
this is a...
for for you...
teachers?...
all?...

So what...
Halloween...
you go out...
meaghan...
baby — i...
is Shannon...
Is Lynn...
belly too?...
going to h...
You sure...
a bussy...
few year...
i'D hav...
and that...

...for now.

Just remember Jarrett
please — i love you
and miss you very
very VERY MUCH!

If you want to write
to me — write me a
letter and Grandpa can
mail it for you. I
hope you do.

I love you
Jarrett

Mommy

CHAPTER 3
SKIPPING A GENERATION

Rise and shine. It's an exciting day for you, Ja.

The room was covered in green-tinted wallpaper and wall-to-wall green carpeting. Green was my grandmother's favorite color. This had been Steve's bedroom. Once he left for college, my grandparents had the room done over for Shirley to live in. She often reminded me of that over the years. Not in a mean way, just in a Shirley kind of way.

Yeah, this was going to be my room, but I wanted you to have it. In case you were wondering why everything is green, that's why I mention it.

70

Life on Brookline Street soldiered on—now with a little kid in the mix. After raising five children, Joe and Shirl had been getting ready to be empty nesters. Their youngest two, Holly and Lynn, were growing into their teens, and high school graduation was in sight for both girls.

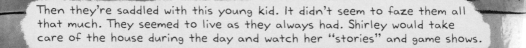

Then they're saddled with this young kid. It didn't seem to faze them all that much. They seemed to live as they always had. Shirley would take care of the house during the day and watch her "stories" and game shows.

From the outside, it looked fairly idyllic. But some nights, Joe wouldn't come home at the end of the day, and Shirley and I would eat in silence. Then the front door would open and the smell of alcohol would fill the house.

Nightmares continued to haunt my nights.

My grandparents would tell me later that there were many mornings when they found me asleep just outside their door.

81

I treasured that time with my mother. I hadn't seen her in so long.

At the end of the day, I thought my mother would be coming home with us.

I'm sorry, Ja. But I have to stay here. It's just for a little while, though. Then I'll be home again.

You'll see.

Don't cry now. I didn't even give you my gift.
Do you like him?
He's going to need a name.
I'll name him Snow Cone. Because he's a polar bear.
Makes perfect sense to me!
Come on now, Jarrett. It's getting late.
I love you so much.
I want you to come home with us.

Snow Cone was the closest thing that I had to her. I treated that bear like it was real. Like it had feelings. I dressed him up in clothes that I grew out of.

I kept him by me at all times. We were like Christopher Robin and Winnie the Pooh, but instead of the Hundred Acre Woods, we had the empty lot next to our house.

All of Joe and Shirl's kids had gone to Gates Lane. It went all the way through eighth grade, so Lynn and Holly had only left a few years prior to my arrival in kindergarten. It was an old building, built in the late 1800s. The school library was in the basement, across from the cafeteria. Well, the kitchen. There was no actual cafeteria to eat in, so we ate in our classrooms. The art room was up in the attic.

Mrs. Alisch

I had some great teachers there. Like Mrs. Alisch, my first-grade teacher who smelled like perfume, and Mrs. Roy, my second-grade teacher who smelled like cigarettes and mimeograph paper.

I didn't play sports at all, so come recess I was a loner.

I thought at that point in my life that my mother would be back home. But she never did return. She wasn't talked about much around the house. There would be phone calls from her once in a great while. Mostly she'd write. She was an incredibly talented artist. She'd make her own cards and draw my favorite cartoon characters. We had this thing where we would go back and forth—I'd request a cartoon from her and then she'd request one back from me. I didn't know where the letters and drawings were going to—my grandfather would take them and mail them for me.

Wednesday-
Hi Kiddo-
Here's your Donald Duck. Before I forget
you can draw me Woodstock or a Smurf.
Nothing new to write about. I'm starting a
Typing class next week. I don't like typing,
but maybe I'll find a new job that will
make me RICH!!
Your hair must be getting pretty light from
the sun.
There's not much to say right now. Plus it's
almost 1:00 am and I'm pretty tired. So
even though this is a very short letter, I'm
sending it along with the picture. I'll be
talking to you probably before you get this
letter anyway.
I love you + miss you a lot.
Love
Mom.
MY HEART SKIPS A BEAT...
i love you Jarrett...
this much!
Dear Jarrett,
How are ya doing buddy??
How is your cold? Better i
hope ♥ You said your favorite
colors are RED and black so here
they are. I'm O.K. and by the
way, your letter was great. So
was the picture of Rusty. Glad
to hear you're doing so well in
school too. How are you doing
with your new scooter - tell
me more about it. Are you
still working on your computer?
Well kiddo, let me go get this
in the mail. I'll write a longer
letter real soon O.K.
Love you lots... MOMMY

My mom didn't even come around for my birthdays.

She never came by when Grandma would bake a lasagna and Joe would pick up an ice-cream cake from the Carvel down the street.

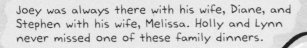

Joey was always there with his wife, Diane, and Stephen with his wife, Melissa. Holly and Lynn never missed one of these family dinners.

But I always felt the void that Leslie's absence created.

There was this one birthday party my mom threw for me, though. She just turned up unannounced one day and took me out.

But, Mom, it's June. It isn't even anywhere near my birthday.

Just go with it.

I never get to be around for any of these things.

Besides, Grandma and Grandpa never throw you a party with any of your friends.

She was right. With my birthday being so close to Christmas, Joe and Shirl just didn't see the point. So we called some of the kids in my class.

Is this the birthday boy?!

Well, actually—

It sure is! Right, kiddo?!

Great! Come on this way! Your guests should be arriving any moment, I am sure.

Happy birthday to me!

It was all a lie, but I had to admit—it was a lot of fun. This fake McDonald's birthday party? It's the only party that I ever had with friends throughout my entire childhood.

And it was really nice having my mom there. I liked being able for her to meet some of my friends, and for them to meet her.

But it would be a long time before any of them—or I—saw her again. Because just as quickly as she'd reappeared, she was gone again.

One day, Holly just couldn't take it any longer. She threw all of her clothes in a trash bag, picked up Ashley, and moved across the street—where her boyfriend, Brian, lived.

Looks like they're going to break ground on the neighbors' house.

What neighbors?

We're getting new neighbors.

Where?

In the lot next door.

Well, they're building a house. You'll have to make friends with the kid who's moving in.

But that's where I play!

We hear they have a kid your age.

Over the next few months, I watched from my bedroom as the empty lot transformed into a house. And then a few days before third grade started, a family moved in.

That's what makes him so cool. He doesn't need superpowers. He's smart and he's strong and he invented all those cool batgadgets.

Pat and I were both in Ms. Turner's third-grade classroom.

GATES LANE
WORCESTER
MASS
GR3
RM16
1986

105

THE OWL WHO THOUGHT HE WAS THE BEST FLYER

J KROSOCZKA

In third grade, we wrote our own books based on Greek myths. Mrs. Turner taught us about brainstorming and organizing our ideas. I loved that project.

We also had an author visit our school. He wrote this series called Rotten Ralph.

I just didn't understand why Rusty had turned on me like that.
I took care of his every need, and he was ready to ditch me.

Wednesday nite

Dear Jarrett –

Hi kiddo! What's up? Called you Sunday but Holly said you were in Canada. How was your trip?

Here is that paper with the California raisins I told you about. Also, 2 cards I made of them.

I made these 2 scarfs for you and Rusty to wear up at the beach to keep warm. I thought it would be cute to make one for him too. Hope you like it!

How's school going? Good I hope. I want you to be careful halloween night. And check all your candy before you eat it. I Hope you have a really, really good time. I'm working on your Halloween card — I'll be late but I didn't forget.

Well let me get this stuff ready to mail tomorrow. I'll probably call you this weekend.

Love Mom

P.S. Finished your Halloween card – Hope you like it

So, you and your hamster have matching scarves?

Yup. My mother knit them herself.

Cool, cool...

Pat never asked me about where my mother was. I wouldn't have had an answer if he'd asked. My grandparents never told me.

Wherever she was, she'd taken the time to knit me and Rusty matching scarves. And that was really cool.

They decided to walk in.
Tom Tomatoe Went in first
without knowing there would be
a trapdoor.

CHAPTER 4
DISCLOSURE

You are all a bunch of fecking assholes!
It wasn't unusual to hear foul language coming from my grandmother. And when she was really drunk, sometimes she'd turn that language against me and Grandpa.
You two just love each other, don't you? Best frrrriends. You love yer grandfather more than you love me.
No, I love you both the same.
I'm going to fecking bed.

That recurring dream? The one with the monsters in the field? It kept coming. The monsters, they kept coming for me.

I'd stare them right in the eyes and they would freeze until I needed to turn and look at another monster to freeze.

And it kept happening.

Again and again, around and around I would spin until they were on top of me.

We left the next week. My grandfather took me on all of the rides while my grandmother cheered us on.
Hey, Donald! Come pose for a photo, will ya?!
I could have picked out Mickey ears, but I was all about the Goofy hat.

We laughed a lot on that trip.
Which is why I was so taken off guard when, not long after we returned home, my grandfather called another family meeting.

My grandfather didn't say much beyond that.

But over the years, the truth would all reveal itself to me.

My mother started using when she was just thirteen years old. Joe and Shirl tried to help her, but things just got worse and worse. For everyone.

Mom & DAD,

(I Don't know who Did it)

I know you Don't beleive me Mom.

I Don't blame either of you. I love

you both really I Do, even if I Don't

show it. <u>Please</u> Don't come look for

me. I'll be back in a couple of DAys,

~~maybe~~ maybe even tomorrow. I need time

to think. You Do to. Ya know Mom,

I think you should know by now that

th___ ea___ boar Di___ ___

___e ___ Don't ___

___ It's

___now ___

Things were bad at home—things were bad wherever Leslie went. She would run away from home and then turn up again without warning.

...now.

I'll be probly tomorrow. If not tomorrow — sometime this week. I know you both probly think I'm crazy or something. I'm not — I'm just a mixed up on a couple of things. The time I take now will help me

Remember I DO love you.

You I'm sorry.

Love,
Leslie

You. Don
kinda scared. So,

My grandfather got her an apartment downtown when she was sixteen, thinking that would help her. It didn't. It only made it worse.

She'd steal anything to sell it for heroin. She'd walk into a store with a trash bag, fill it with batteries, and then run out of the store—selling the batteries on the black market to fuel her addiction.

She'd shoplift from TJ Maxx and then have her unsuspecting baby sisters return the merchandise for cash. They had no idea the goods were stolen. They thought they were just running errands for their big sister.

And Leslie would steal from Joe and Shirl—all the time. One time, Grandma had her purse sitting out on the kitchen table. Leslie grabbed it and ran. Shirley chased her down the street, but it was no use. She had to go out and get a brand-new license and cancel her credit cards.

That's why my grandmother was always hiding her purse in cabinets. But the most heartbreaking moment came when Shirley was washing the dishes one night. She took her wedding ring off and placed it to the side of the sink. Leslie knocked her down, grabbed the ring, and disappeared into the night.

On nights that she would return, she wasn't let into the house. Leslie banged on the door until it cracked. The only time that Leslie didn't use was when she got pregnant with me. I was lucky not to be born addicted to heroin. And I was told that—often. But after I came into the world, Leslie started using again. And again and again. My grandfather swooped in, gaining legal custody of me so that I wouldn't become a ward of the state. Leslie tried halfway homes, attempting to recover. But nothing worked. She always went back to that poison.

I knew in that moment, when my grandfather told me the plain truth, that life wouldn't be the same for me. It didn't change the circumstances, but it shifted my perspective.

Just say no.

This is your brain.

Pat was the only friend I had that I could trust with this information.

CHAPTER 5
PEN TO PAPER

KNOCK
KNOCK

Hey,
kiddo.

Hey, Grandpa.

Your grandmother
and I have been
thinking...and it's
up to you...

...but we'd like to send you to take classes at the Worcester Art Museum.

Really?!

Really. You can choose any class you want. I earmarked the page for kids 12 and up.

Doesn't matter how much it costs or what day it's on—we'll get you there.

At the time, public funding for art in the Worcester public schools kept getting slashed and I went from having art once a week to once a month to not at all. Art was the only thing that I had any sort of interest in. I wasn't about to join Little League like all of my friends.

Okay, either me or Lynn or Holly will pick you up when the class is done.

145

First things first, I want you all to come around and check out these comics I brought to share.

Now, I know you all have your superhero comics, but I want to introduce you to some really different things here. Some really bizarre and different stuff? Important work.

Mark brought in all sorts of comics, things I never would have looked at otherwise, some comics that I probably wouldn't even have been allowed to pick up at the comic book shop.

Every week, we'd come into class and Mark would introduce us to a new cartoonist and then play super-weird underground music while we worked on our own comics.

He had us work on Bristol board and use India ink, and he taught us how to use Nib pens and draw with a brush like real cartoonists.

Okay, now—the BIG project for the semester, guys—and this is serious, now, is that we just got the green light to make our own 'zine.

You're all going to have your own mini comic in this collection, and, AND it's going to be sold at That's Entertainment comics over on Park Ave.

But, BUT here's the thing. You need to get your work in on time. And you need to put a solid effort into the art. I'm not going to put my name or the museum's name on work that isn't up to snuff.

Week after week, I'd get to Mark's classroom and I would work my butt off. I didn't have the motivation to work this hard on my regular coursework for school, but this was everything I wanted in life. One week, I brought in a book that I had just read—How to Draw Comics the Marvel Way. I couldn't wait to tell Mark all about it. I wanted nothing more than to be a better cartoonist. I figured he'd be super proud of me. To me, this book was my ticket to cartoonist stardom.

You read this?

The entire book! There's this one part—

Forget everything you learned.

One thing that book did have that I paid attention to was a supplies list. And on top of that list was a drafting table. If I was to become a professional cartoonist, I needed a good table to work on.

CC LOWELL

This one should suit your needs, but if you want to spend a little more money, this one over here—

No, this one will have everything I'll need.

Later that night, I taped that fortune to the top-left corner of my desk and started working on my contribution to Mark Lynch's comics anthology.

With my comics, I was in charge of what happened. I could escape fully into these worlds that I created. But the real world, it kept coming for me, and I controlled none of it.

This is a big deal for your mother. You know that, right?

Friendly's does have great ice cream.

Sure.

If Leslie can prove to her probation officer that she can hold down a job, she'll move back to Worcester.

She can do it. I know she can. How hard can it be to scoop ice cream?

Well, yeah, she can do that. But she needs to keep clean while she does.

You ready?

Always ready for ice cream.

Table for two, please.

Hey, Dad!
Hey, Ja!

C'mon! I'll put you in our best booth. Would you like a dinner menu or just ice cream?

I'll take a pistachio in a cup.

Cone Head sundae, please!

Well, look at you! Don't even need to look at the menu!

Okay, fine. Ja, I got this for you.

Cool, thanks!

See you soon, kiddo. I love you.

My mom gave me this crystal thing. When you held it up to the light, it created a rainbow.

We said our goodbyes, and my grandfather was awfully quiet on the way home.

I didn't hear from my mother much in the following days. And my grandparents didn't mention her.

Then one day, some months later, he slammed the newspaper down on the kitchen table.

Goddamnit.

Well, if you were wondering where your mother has been, her name is here in the paper.
They found her O.D.'d face down on the pavement.

There it was—right there in the newspaper's court records, just a few pages away from the comics page.

My mother's name.

Our family's name.

Printed for all to see.

Leslie Krosoczka, 39, of Worcester, was discovered unconscious of a suspected overdose on the corner of Piedmont St. and Main St. Krosoczka was taken to St. Vincent Hospital where she was treated and charged with ... of narcotics. A court date has been set for

Grandpa got an old pool table and put it in the basement. I think he just wanted to make sure that my friends were coming over to our house and I wasn't going out and getting into trouble.

C'mon, man! You have to go! It's going to be so much fun.

What's the point of me going to a dance, Pat, if I don't know how to dance?!

It's not about dancing. Nah, it's about hanging out. And we only have a few dances left this year—you've got to go to one of them. There's no reason to be *embarrassed*.

What if a girl asks me to dance?!?

Then you just dance with her! Drrr! All you have to do is put your hand on her hips and sway to the music.

C'mon, I'll teach you the Running Man. It's simple.

click

New experiences and new revelations continued to unfold in all aspects of my life.

So what's it gonna be?

Southern Comfort Manhattan, dry with a twist, rocks on the side.

HA!!! Well, I know that's what your grandparents will have. How about a Coke, sweetie?

Yes, please.

Alright, I'll be right back with your drinks and I'll take your order.

I had my grandparents' drink order memorized. Ice on the side so they could fit more liquor in the glass.

So...I ran into your father today.

This was the first time anybody had ever mentioned anything to me about my father. Like, it was never even acknowledged that a father even existed before this point.

Do you want to know his name?

Sure.

I had never given much thought to who my father was. And knowing his name wasn't going to change that.

Meanwhile, my mother returned to my life, in the form of another visiting day. I was equally as unenthused.

I really don't want to see her.

You'll be glad that you did.

We're here to see Leslie Krosoczka.

I'm going to need to see your identification, and you'll need to fill out these forms.

I hate her.

She's your mother, and don't use the word "hate." That's a terrible word.

I strongly dislike the woman who gave birth to me. Is that better?

Look, you might not want to see her, but she wants to see you. And maybe seeing you is going to help her out. Think about that.

Right this way, please.

Stacey.

Hey, Tina! C'mere! I want you to meet my son, Jarrett.

Hey! Leslie tells me you go to Gates Lane School in Worcester. You know Mariah Lopez?

Uh, yeah. She's in all of my classes.

That's my daughter. Tell her I said hello when you see her, okay?

I didn't know how I would broach that subject with Mariah. Nobody knew Mariah's mom was in a halfway home and they certainly didn't know that my mom was there, too. Plus, I was afraid that Mariah would punch me.

Our kids are in the same class! Too bad Jarrett has a girlfriend— we coulda set them up.

So, you get out soon? Will you make it to my eighth-grade graduation in June?

I'll be done with this place soon, but not soon enough, pal. I'm sorry that I won't be out by June. I'm going to miss it.

But you'll take lots of pictures, right? And we'll always have high school graduation! I'll be there for sure! I won't miss that, I promise.

Leslie, your time is almost up.

What's this thing about an eighth-grade graduation dinner?

It's nothing. Parents aren't going to that.

Says here in the invitation that they are.

Well, I mean, none of my friends' parents are going.

So you guys don't have to go to that. It's not worth the trouble.

That, of course, was a lie. Here's the truth: I was embarrassed to have my grandparents there. They'd be so much older than all of the other kids' parents. And I'd managed to mostly not blend my family life and my school life.

Oh. I see.

So Grandma and I will skip it, then.

I had never seen my grandparents look so hurt.

But all the parents are definitely coming to the graduation ceremony.

We'll see.

Eighth-grade graduation came. We all sang the songs that our music teacher had been practicing. "Coming Out of the Dark" by Gloria Estefan, "When the Children Cry" by White Lion, and the remixed version of "Lean on Me."

Mrs. Alisch was retiring, and I was selected to be the student to deliver a farewell speech to her.

Then, one by one, we were called up on stage to receive our diplomas—even some of the kids who probably hadn't passed all their classes. I'm sure Mr. Johnson just wanted them to move on from Gates Lane.

I was able to convince my grandparents to attend the dinner afterwards. They sat with Pat's parents. I didn't even mind that they sat back and watched me and my classmates all hit the dance floor.

I met a lot of my friends' parents that night. Some were old, some were young. Some were single, some were divorced. I was mad at my mother for not being there for me that day, but at the same time, I was glad that she wasn't there. Every adult at the dinner had a hand in raising all of the eighth-grade graduates, and I had my true parents there.

THE NAPOLEON

is animated character

...sed
...ur-
...emy
...eries
...side-
...d pro-
who is

...st be-
...watch-
...nose to
...n apart
...Gates
...ttended
...useum
seventh
...n in the
...l and is
...the direc-

...od entails
...wednesday
...m. at the
...Krosoczka
...there since
...l him to en-
...s. Since then
...n animation
...and is pres-
...d comic book

Jarrett Krosoczka skillfully creates his animated charact...

class under the direction of teacher Mr. Mark Lynch.

Krosoczka also explained that at the Worcester Art Museum they have a professional animation camera. The professional camera is able to record 100 pictures in 30 seconds, which breaks down to nine drawings per second. Krosoczka discovered that he can virtually do the same with his camcorder, by slowing down the proce-du... He is able to record four drawing...

per second.

Through...
what he consi...
Krosoczka h...
cartoon.

He first created the storyboar...
storyboard includes his character sketches and the lines that his voice crew will speak. After he completes his sketches in pencil, he outlines them with a black marker. Then the voice crew colors in the drawings with Crayola

...ny...
channel and is...
for anyone when a video tape...
plied. "I'm going to keep my fingers crossed and hope for the best," is Krosoczka's present attitude.

ge of c...

...cher
...e is a strange
...he ways of its
...nd strange to
..., however, the
...ught to America
...students. These
...homes of variou
...ool.
...e trip was to he
...nts better th
...akagami, the
...chaperone a
...ave few opport
...ve English sp
...anguage is so
...nly way we wi
...e immersed i

The Boston Globe
Scholastic Art
Awards

Honorable Mention
to

Jarrett Krosoczka

1994

THE SCHOLASTIC
ART & WRITING AWARDS

Conducted Nationally by Scholastic Corporation

Calendar

BLOCKBUSTER®
T-120
HIGH STANDARD
BLANK TAPE

VHS

Dude's World

Attention • Only one side of the video tape can be used.
• Removal of the safety tab will prevent accidental erasure.

Insert this side into recorder ◄► Do not touch the tape inside

CHAPTER 6
HARD WORK

We'd sleep over at each other's houses and then sneak out to meet up with girls at Webster Square Plaza.

WEBSTER SQ PLAZA

I thought maybe everything would stay exactly the same once we all got to high school. But then Stacey came by my house with a bag.

I'm breaking up with you.

In that bag? Every stuffed animal I'd ever won her and every note I'd ever handed to her in class. I was devastated.

While most of my friends went to South High, I was shipped off to Holy Name. And Gates Lane School was torn down to make way for a new, more modern building.

When I was a kid, Lynn had tried to warn me, "If you don't start playing sports now, by the time you get to high school, you'll be a total dork." Now the prophecy was coming true. I started high school as an unathletic kid with braces, glasses, and skin that wouldn't clear.

I'd managed to build up a great spot in the social hierarchy of school back at Gates Lane. But now I was starting from scratch.

En nombre de Padre, de Hijo y de espiritu santo. Amén.

Seeing the sports teams at Holy Name didn't exactly make me want to take part. Our mascot was The Napoleon—as in Napoleon Bonaparte. The school had been founded by French nuns, and the story was that the basketball team was "small but mighty." At games, cheerleaders would proclaim, "Go, NAPS!" Lame.

BOYS' LOCKER ROOM ▷

In a terrible stroke of luck, I had gym class with the upperclassmen to accommodate taking art as an elective.

I took solace in Mr. Shilale's art class. It almost made it worth it to deal with those Neanderthals in gym class.

Hello, class. We are going to start today as we start every day, with a thought of the day. "The most visible creators are those artists whose medium is life itself. The ones who express the inexpressible — without brush, hammer, clay, or guitar. They neither paint nor sculpt. Their medium is simply being. Whatever their presence touches has increased life. They see, but don't have to draw...Because they are the artists of being alive..." — Donna J. Stone.

Something to think about, class. Now please take out your still lifes and get ready to work!

I just don't see the point in still lifes. This isn't the kind of art I want to make.

This is pretty dull.

Ah, yes. But it's important! Even the world's greatest abstract artists learned how to draw realistically before they could pick apart the imagery. What kind of art are you two most interested in?

I really want to paint, like Georgia O'Keeffe or something like that.

I want to be a cartoonist. Maybe for comic strips or comic books.

Well, stick with these projects that I'm giving you. It will help you out in the long run.

If you say so. I don't see how drawing this bowl of fruit on top of a bunch of boxes is going to help me draw comics.

You're going to have to draw cityscapes and environments, right? Your imagined worlds will come to life so much more strongly if you get a good foundation in learning to be a draftsman through observation. Keep at it. You'll be great!

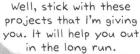

Mr. Shilale may have had a point, but I still just wanted to tell stories with my drawings. So I would twist his still-life assignments to make them more interesting to me.
I couldn't rely on just the 45 minutes of daily sanctuary that Mr. Shilale's class gave me. I needed to make friends. So I did it the only way I knew how.

"There is no such thing as a mistake, only a correction." Do you know who said that quote, class?

I did.

Now, class, your next assignment will be to draw an editorial cartoon for the <u>Telegram & Gazette</u>'s student contest. Perhaps one of yours will be published?

I was beyond excited. I got right to work. I ended up submitting four different ideas.

Ugh! Brownnoser.

I'm not looking to get brownie points with Shilale. I want to get my work published.

Pfft! Whatever.

I have some good news, class! A piece from a Holy Name student was chosen for publication in the <u>Telegram & Gazette</u>!

And it wasn't an upperclassman from Art 2, 3, or 4. It is from a freshman.

Jarrett! Your cartoon will run in Sunday's edition of the paper!

Every weekend morning, my grandparents' eldest, Joey, would stop in with the newspaper on his way to the gym.

Hey, Ma. Hey, Pa.

Soon after my work made its debut in the city paper, my first cartoon appeared in the school paper, too.

I really wanted to go to South High to be with all of my friends, but I also really liked the idea of getting to be the cartoonist for the school newspaper and get that recognition with every issue. I'd have to just continue to hang with Pat and our crew on the weekends.

Mrs. Casey?

Why, hello, Mr. Krosoczka.

I'll take the job. I'm going to stay at Holy Name.

Well, good. Because we have more issues coming up, and see that empty bulletin board across the hall? I'd like for you to paint a mural of our school mascot on it.

Hard work was something that my grandfather talked a lot about. He'd grown up during the Great Depression and always shared stories about what it was like for him back in the day.

I started working when I was nine. My mother bought fruits and vegetables from an old man named Isaac, so I asked him for a job one summer. I just wanted to work. I'd meet Isaac at the stables every morning at six. I'd help him hitch up his horse to the carriage and we'd ride into the square, where we bought produce from the farmers.

We'd then ride through the neighborhoods, and people would shout out their orders from their windows. I'd run the baskets of fruit and vegetables to each house. We'd get the horse back to the stable around eight at night. On a good day, I'd take home fifty cents.

To make a coupla extra bucks, I'd polish shoes. Made my own box to carry my supplies in and for folks to put their feet up on.

And of course, Joe loved reflecting on his ill-fated necktie business.

It was his out-of-the-box thinking that led him to revolutionize the ball-valve industry.

The factory grew to have about 125 employees at its height. They received contracts to manufacture valve balls for the U.S. government that were about three feet tall and weighed 4,000 pounds.

It gave Joe something to boast about, so he had T-shirts printed up.

We've got the biggest balls in the industry.

Joe put me to work at the shop. It was a family business. My uncles, Joey and Stephen, helped run things in the main office, and at different points Leslie, Lynn, and Holly all worked there in some capacity. Joe put me to work on the assembly line, next to Auntie Helen. She was my great-aunt, Joe's older sister.

Yah doin' it wrong!

Hurry it up, will ya?!

You know that story 'bout Ewey Guey? The worm that cross the train tracks and then...Ewey Guey! HAHA!

As I went through the motions of working on the machines, I dreamed of the comics I'd make when I got home.

209

CHAPTER 7
GHOSTS

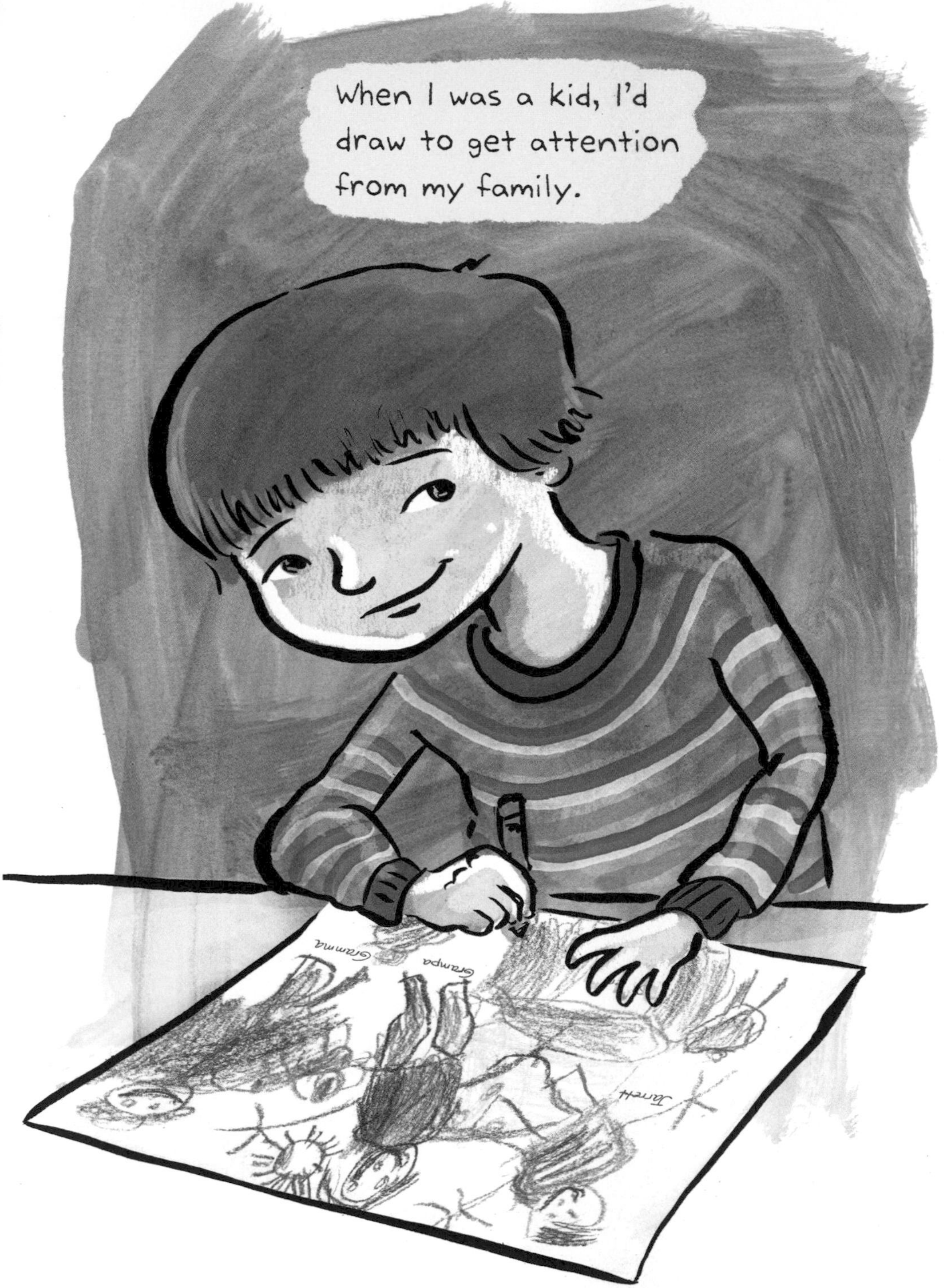
When I was a kid, I'd draw to get attention from my family.

In junior high, I drew
to impress my friends.

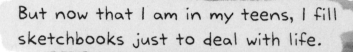

But now that I am in my teens, I fill sketchbooks just to deal with life.

To survive.

You spend time dealing with the ghosts of the past, they'll continue to haunt you.
The problem is, the ghosts wouldn't leave me alone, I needed to face them.

On the evening of Christmas, it was usually just me, Joe and Shirley. Christmas Eve was always the big Krosoczka family party, and then Joey, Steve, Lynn, and Holly would be with their new families and in-laws on Christmas Day. But this Christmas? We had a guest...

SLAM!

Hellllllloooo!

Jesus Christ, would it kill you to call and say that you're gonna be late?

You don't need to wait on me, Ma.

Don't worry, we didn't.

Hi, Dad.

Hi, Les.

So, was Santa good to you, Ja?

221

Well, we go way, way back. But we just met up again at the clinic.

I think he had a thing for me back in the day. Can ya blame him?

We ended up in the same release program and he finally built up the nerve to ask me out.

Ah. Romance at the clinic.

What about you, kiddo? You have a special someone?

No.

So...you still drawing? I hear you got a cartoon in the paper.

Yup.

The air always seemed to get sucked out of the room whenever Leslie stepped into it. At least we had my grandmother to lighten the mood.

REALLY?!

Dude. She doesn't know you exist. You've never spoken to her.

Those Holy Name girls, man. We gotta get to this game. There's gotta be somebody we could hitch a ride with.

Well, there is one person I could ask...

Hey, bub! Somebody ordered a taxi?

So this is your mom?

It was unsettling to see my mother with a boyfriend. It's not that I thought she should be with my father—I didn't even know that guy. But I had never seen her with a dedicated anyone, and the men that I did see come into her life had always mistreated her.

228

My grandfather wanted Leslie to get out of her downtown apartment, so he bought a house around the corner from us. My grandmother wasn't on board—she listed all of the things they'd already spent money on to help Leslie get back on her feet. Nothing ever seemed to work. But this time, my grandfather insisted, would be different. He would collect rent from his daughter and her boyfriend.

Just put that last box over there, Ja.

Alright. See you.

Hey, before you leave, I want you to know that Miguel, he's good to me.

He's getting treatment, just like me.

He used to be one of the biggest drug dealers in the city, but those days are behind him.

So he's motivated.

Ha! Yeah. You'll like him. He's not like the other guys I've had around.

Miguel and I are on this road to recovery together. He had a tough childhood, watched his mother burn to death.

Jesus.

We all have our baggage. I mean, when I was your age, Grandma and Grandpa kicked me out of the house. We all have our stories of how we came to be, ya know?

That must have been weird.

It was great at first. I had my freedom. Grandpa got me my own place to make life easier for everyone. Ma's drinking was out of control. It was nothing but yelling and screaming between the two of us. I couldn't take it anymore. Nobody could take it anymore. I had started using before I moved out, but things got worse fast once I got my own place.

It was strange enough to have my mother close by. It wasn't absence anymore, but it wasn't a cure for absence, either.

Another shift happened more by accident. I needed my birth certificate for a school trip. When I saw it for the first time, I also saw my father's last name for the first time.

Hennessy.

I had to laugh to myself. Turns out, I was just as Irish as Pat.

As the absence of this information turned into a presence, I struggled to know what to do with it. When my grandparents were out, I'd grab the phone book and look up the full name: Richard Hennessy. There were a few listed. One of them was my father.

There was a part of me that thought about calling each one. I imagined reaching my father's house and disrupting whatever perfect little life he was leading.

But I never called.

You know, when you were born, we were going to name you Oscah. Then your name woulda been "Oscah Krosoczka." HA!

It was a tired old joke that I heard at least once a month. But I humored my grandfather.

HA!

I love you.

I love you more.

I love you more than that.

I'd like to buy a vowel, Pat...

I was raised to always say "I love you" before leaving the house. It was something my grandfather had done with his parents and he instilled it in me. Because (he said) you never know when you're going to see your loved ones again.

There was one hangout spot that we didn't need to worry about getting a ride to. But we did need to make sure that nobody spotted us as we slipped passed Christo's restaurant and sneaked into the woods.

For my grandparents' wedding anniversary, I painted them a portrait. I worked super hard on it. I didn't paint much, so that was new to me, but I was determined to make something that they could be proud of. I worked on it for weeks. I even spent the money to get it custom-framed at C.C. Lowell.

Today is a big day, right? Happy anniversary!

Oh, you're so full of it.

Forty-five years with this honey bunny. Nothing but bliss!

I know it couldn't have been easy for Shirl to have such a looker like me on her arm. But it's like I always said: If ya got it, flaunt it!
Yeah, that's the trouble with you. You always flaunt it whether you got it or not!
Well, I have a present for both of you!

When you're raised by your grandparents, death is just a part of the regular household conversation. Anytime you took a photo with my grandma, she'd say, "If that comes out good, put it in the paper." She wanted to ensure that her friends saw a flattering photo in her obituary. My grandfather started talking to me about his will before I hit double digits. I grew up knowing that Joseph and Shirley, the two people who raised me, wouldn't live well into my adulthood.

It looks sharp!

When I go, have them put me closer to the street so that I can sneak out at night.

JOSEPH D. KROSOCZKA
1928 +
HIS WIFE
SHIRLEY R. OLSON
1926 +

You're such a bastard.

Still. I wasn't prepared when my grandfather said, "Oh, hey, they put the stone in," on the way home from Coney Island Hot Dog. Sure enough, we pulled into Hope Cemetery and there it was: a tombstone with my grandparents' birth years etched in, and a space waiting for the years of their deaths.

Can we go now?

You know, Jarrett, someday I'm going to be gone.

And if you remember any of the lessons that I taught you in this lifetime, I hope that you remember to work hard. No matter what job you have, in everything you do—give it your all.

I will.

And when I'm gone, I'm sure everyone will be saying, "Thank God that bitch is dead."

They won't be saying that.

Well, you'd better not!

Let's get home.

Jesus, hurry up, Joe! I gotta pee!

Jarrett, grab the mail, will ya?

Yup.

Bills. Junk mail. And a letter that had a return address that stopped me in my tracks

I recognized the name and the return address immediately.

It was my father.

1995

Holy Name Central Catholic High School · Worcester · Mass.

...t,

... I really have no idea
... reaction to this letter is
... be You certainly have a
... your feelings whatever they
... have no good reason for
... all this time without
... you. My biggest mistake
... not opening a line of
... ... I am sure that over
... you could have used
... life and that is
well ... denied. I'm sure that under the
you ... circumstances I could not have
... been the person you needed.
ap ... For the neglect you have suffered
to h ... I can do nothing but
comm ... apologize. I can't change what
dese ... happened. I see now if I could
... go back and undo it I would—
but of course I can't. What has
happened to you has been unfair.
I hope that your life is going

... touch and know ...
very open to that If there is
... thing you need from me, I am
... that also. If, on the other
... no desire to communicate
... and that also.
Sincerely,

CHRISTMAS 29 USA

CHAPTER 8
LOST AND FOUND

259

That summer, I got my driver's license. I tooled around in my grandmother's 1984 Buick Century and I loved it. No cassette deck or power windows, just pure freedom.

WHILE AT A TOLL BOOTH...

SUDDENLY....

OH NO, THE HUGE VAN IN FRONT OF ME IS BACKING U

BANG

RISD DRAWING → BICYCLE

My senior year began and I got to work on my portfolio for college. I had my sights set on Rhode Island School of Design. RISD required three original drawings to accompany your portfolio—a drawing of a bicycle, a drawing of an interior or exterior space, and then a drawing of our choice.

Mr. Shilale advised me to not include a lot of cartooning work, saying they'd be looking for work from observation. But how could I not include work that was totally and completely me?

I also volunteered at Camp Sunshine that fall, a camp for kids with cancer and their families, and it totally changed my life.

I was assigned to the Orfao family—a mom and three kids. The youngest, Eric, had leukemia. Imagine that: a four-year-old with leukemia. The oldest, Jason, told me I had been like a big brother to them that week. That really hit me.

On my desk, I kept a photo of me and those kids from camp. The more I looked at it, the more I couldn't help but think—what if I had a brother and sister?

Like, what if my father went on to have more kids? He didn't mention anything about me having siblings in his letter...but if they were out there? What if they were out there? I would never know unless I wrote my father back.

I mailed the letter without telling anybody about it.

Richard.
It's been nearly 17 years and in that time, not a single birthday card, not a single anything from you. I've had an amazing life so far and you've missed it. You haven't been there for a fucking thing. I'm only writing you back because I have one question for you. Do I have a brother or sister through you?

I was obsessive over checking the mail. Day after day, I would look as the temperature dropped.

Then one day, amongst all the junk mail and bills, I saw that familiar return address once again.

But this time, I felt that the envelope had a photo in it.

I was about to see what my father looked like.

SLAM!

For the first time, I was seeing my father's face.

As I was trying to figure out how to deal with my father, Mother's Day came along. Mother's Day was always a difficult holiday to pick out cards for. It was easy to pick out cards for my grandmother. I always made sure that I bought cards that said, "Happy Mother's Day." Never one that said anything about a grandmother.

But for Leslie? None of the cards ever worked.

"You were always there for me..."

"I'm so lucky to have a mother like you..."

"When I reflect on all of the wonderful things you have been to me over the years..."

Nothing ever fit our relationship.

Hallmark didn't make cards that said, "Even though you did all of those drugs, you're still a swell mom!" or cards that read, "Hey, remember all that time you spent in jail and missed, like, every aspect of my childhood?!"

This year, I decided. I wouldn't send Leslie a card. It was my silent protest.

And then, a week later...

Graduation was coming up. As was often the case, I found myself alone in the house. It was a warm spring evening. I don't know what came over me.

I grabbed my father's letter, took the keys to my grandmother's car and I just drove.

I rolled down my window when the Smashing Pumpkins came on the radio and blasted the volume.

I used to be a little boy.

When the sun went down and I still couldn't find his house, I stopped for directions.

He never even told his wife about me.

That's what I kept repeating to myself as I drove home.

I was crushed.

BRRRING

Hello?

Hello. Is, uh, Jarrett there?

This is.

Uh, hi! This is Richard. I'm sorry I missed you just now.

Who's this?

That Monday was a difficult school day to get through. How do you pay attention in class when you know you'll be meeting your father for the first time? Let alone a brother and sister that you never knew about?

I'm home.

Grandma, you're upset. Look, I know that you aren't excited about me meeting him, but he's not going to replace you. Nothing will.

You got a letter from RISD.

This has been opened.

I'm sorry. All these years, I knew your grandparents were giving you what you needed. I never would have been a good father to you.
Not then.

290

That's great! Where?

I don't know. I wanted to go to RISD, but they rejected me. I got into all of my safety schools, so I'll just have to figure out which one.

Wherever you go, they'll be lucky to have you.

Can you draw Batman?

Spider-Man?

Ren and Stimpy?

Ninja Turtles?

Street Sharks?

After I received my diploma, I looked out into the audience. Leslie wasn't there. But even though my mother wasn't there, I still had plenty of family there to cheer me on.

I had spent my entire childhood thinking of myself as an only child, but in reality, I got to be a younger brother to some great siblings and I had a whole bunch of younger cousins that I got to be a big brother and an uncle to all at once.

And you don't need blood ties, because really good friends? They become family.

And then to top it off, I found out that I had a bonus sister and brother literally from another mother.

I always wondered who my father was and I never quite knew where my mother was. But that entire time? I had two incredible parents right there before me the entire time. They just happened to be a generation removed.

They weren't always perfect, but they were mine.
Hey, if this picture comes out good—put it in the paper!

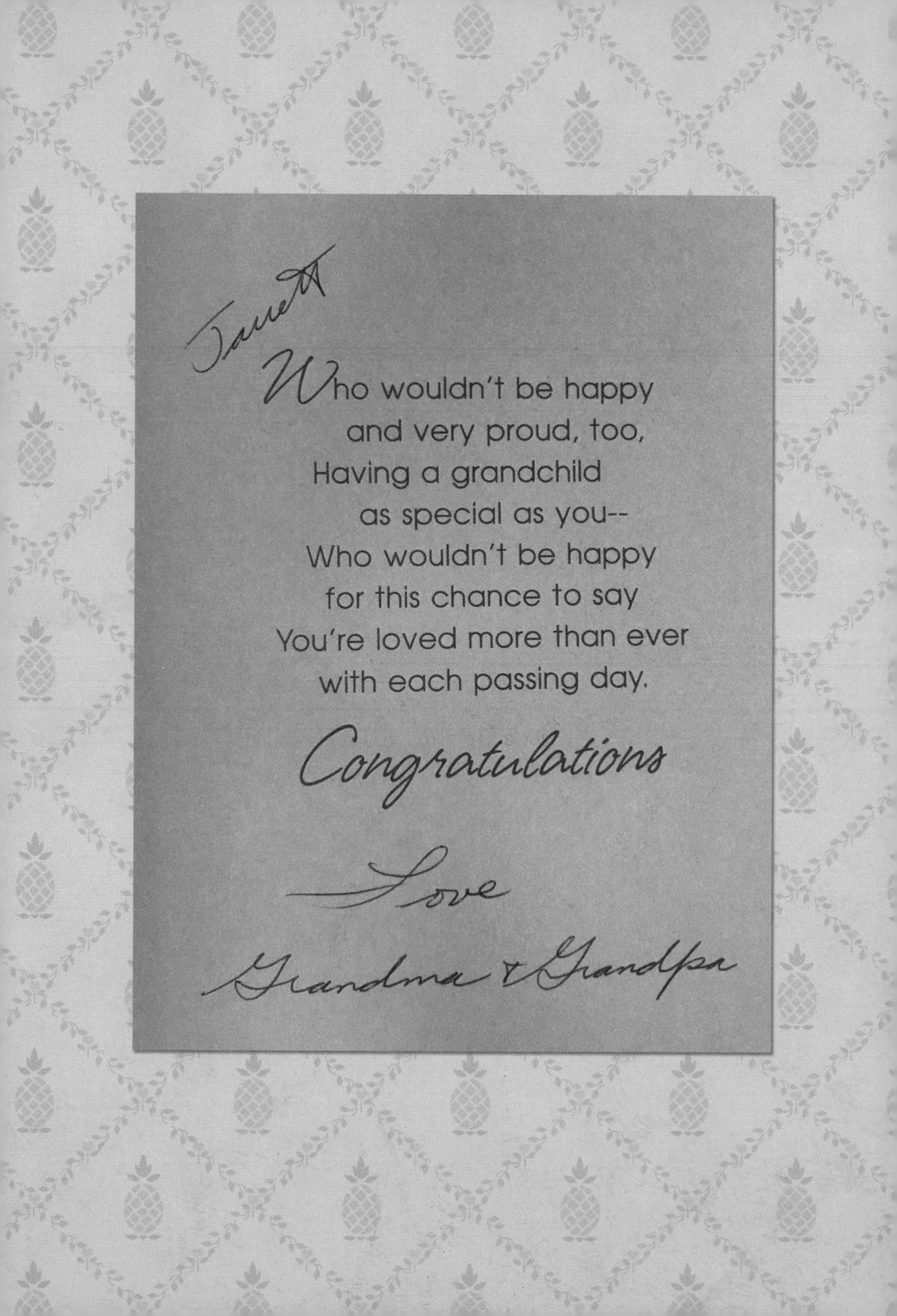

Jarrett

*W*ho wouldn't be happy
and very proud, too,
Having a grandchild
as special as you--
Who wouldn't be happy
for this chance to say
You're loved more than ever
with each passing day.

Congratulations

Love

Grandma & Grandpa

Dear Jarrett—

    I want you to know that I didn't make it to your graduation ceremony because of a health problem. More than anything, I would have loved to have been there to share that moment with you. I have more that needs to be said, but this is not the time. For now, believe me when I say I am <u>so</u> <u>very</u> <u>proud</u> of you and all you have accomplished — and — I love you dearly. There are two things that kept me alive & fighting all these years. One is the love & understanding I have with my father. The other — was you. Enjoy Camp Sunshine.

"I love you this much"

AUTHOR'S NOTE

My mother didn't attend my high school graduation, and I left for college without having any contact with her. That next November, we were reunited at Thanksgiving dinner at my grandparents' house. From there, we actually developed a good relationship. That's not to say that there weren't additional moments of disappointment when Leslie didn't turn up for things when she said she would. That kept happening over and over again. But I came to an understanding of her and I loved her. Over the years, I also developed a strong bond with my brother, Richard, and sister, Maura, and through that, I developed a relationship with my father. It's a friendship that took me by surprise, but one that I am grateful for. At my graduation from Rhode Island School of Design (which I attended as a transfer sophomore), I took a photo with both Leslie and my father Richard—the only photo ever taken of me with both of my birth parents. I treasure that photo.

My grandparents, Joseph and Shirley, were incredibly proud of me—and they said it far before I ever got a book published. But at my first book signing for my first published book (*Good Night, Monkey Boy*, 2001), they were absolutely beaming. The dedication for that book reads *For Grandma and Grandpa, the best parents a kid could ask for.* Growing up, I always knew that the two people who raised me wouldn't live long into my adult life, given their ages. But they both lived to see me succeed with my art. It wasn't an easy decision for them, two people who grew up in the Great Depression, to send their kid to art college. It simply wasn't practical. But they had faith in me, and I worked hard not to disappoint them. More important than that professional accomplishment, both Joe and Shirl also lived to see me fall in love and get engaged. When I sat them down to tell them that things between me and this girl Gina were getting serious, my grandmother handed me her engagement and wedding rings to give to Gina. It's something that she had been saying she would do since I was a kid. She cracked that since Leslie had stolen her original ring, the replacement ring was a nicer diamond, as Joe had been making money then. She also said, "You know, if I didn't like Gina so much, you wouldn't be getting that ring."

Sadly, Shirley died on the weekend of Gina's bridal shower. It was a difficult summer—Leslie's boyfriend had passed away the week before. While we had Joe with us at our wedding, he was never the same after Shirley died. Gina and I welcomed our first child, Zoe, into the world the year after our wedding, and I feel so lucky that she got to meet Joe before his health declined and he suffered from dementia. While Joe's death certificate lists lung cancer, he really did die of a broken heart. Gina and I went on to have two more children—Lucia and Xavier. I so wish that Joe and Shirley could have known my children; they would have absolutely loved them. I now know what Joe meant when he always said that his parents would've loved me.

When you're a kid and a teen, you're not in control of your circumstances. But the beautiful thing about growing up is that you get to create your own reality and your own family. That family might be a group of tight-knit friends, that family might be a spouse and children of your own. But ultimately, your childhood realities do not have to perpetuate themselves into adulthood, not if you don't let them. It for sure takes work.

My grandfather would always tell me, "If you dwell on the ghosts of the past, they'll haunt you." I have found the opposite to be true—if you ignore the ghosts from your past, they'll haunt you and never let go. I should have been in therapy when I was a kid. It would have helped me tremendously. I'm proud to say that I've been in therapy as an adult. My grandparents came up in a different era, when things just weren't talked about.

Addiction is a terrible disease. It took my mother from me slowly and piece by piece until she ultimately suffered a fatal overdose from heroin. She died while I was revising the text for this book. Leslie knew that I was writing a memoir, and expressed hope that perhaps our story could help somebody who might be walking a similar path to the one we had walked. I so wish that she could be holding this finished book and turning the pages.

It was a difficult process, watching my mother take her final downward spiral. At her memorial, I read aloud the letters that she wrote to me while she was in prison. What had become clear to me as I revisited those letters for this book became clear to everyone listening that evening—she loved me so very much. And I was lucky to have that love; it carries me to this day. She was a good person who made bad decisions.

It's futile to think *I wish things had been different.* There is no changing the past. Everything that has happened, no matter how difficult, has made me the person that I am today. Had I not seen how my mother squandered her talent, maybe I wouldn't have been so motivated to make a career out of my art. I am who I am in spite of my mother, but I also am who I am because of her. She taught me to never shy away from expressing my love for family. And our house is one in which we always share our love for one another.

I am now living out my childhood dreams of making a living as an author and an artist, but it is a greater triumph for me to have created a stable, loving home with my wife. I have an amazing spouse who is so supportive and with whom I laugh—a lot. I somehow found Gina just as the foundations of my childhood fell apart. I cherish her and our three children more than words can express. And while Zoe, Lucia, and Xavier will never get to have the time with Grandpa Joe and Grandma Shirley, they do have stories. And stories keep memories alive and people real to us. My kids have weekends at Auntie Holly's and visits with Uncle Steve. Uncle Richie stops by often and they get to see their auntie Maura when she's in town. They also love their uncle Pat, who served in the Coast Guard for twenty-one years. It's pretty amazing to watch my girls and Pat's son hang out—they're like family.

Joe always honored the memory of his late parents, and I now do the same for him and Shirley. After they both passed and I reflected on everything they'd done for me, what stood out the most to me was their decision to send me to classes at the Worcester Art Museum. Art has always been a lifeline for me, and I wanted to extend the same opportunities that I had to kids in my hometown of Worcester, MA. I instituted the Joseph and Shirley Krosoczka Memorial Youth Scholarships at the Worcester Art Museum (or, for short, the Joe and Shirl Art Scholarships). Every year, we raise money to connect kids in unique familial situations to art classes, all in my grandparents' names. It is said that books save lives, but I also say that empty sketchbooks save lives too. I filled up many, and there is no doubt they saved mine.

A NOTE ON THE ART

Whenever my grandfather got dressed up nicely for an event, he would slip a pocket square into the breast pocket of his suit. "Always add a splash of color," he would say as he finished off his sharp look. After he passed away and we were cleaning out his clothes and personal effects, I couldn't get myself to place his pocket squares in the donation pile. My daughter Zoe was eighteen months old at the time. She toddled over to the pocket squares, placed one to her cheek, and said, "Mine!" That pocket square became her security blanket, and to this day she has slept with "Mine" every single night. When we decided that the art for *Hey, Kiddo* would have a limited color palette, my mind immediately went to that pocket square. It's burnt orange.

I grew up on comic strips and comic books—both reading them and making them. My first graphic novel series, Lunch Lady, was an homage to those crisp-lined comics. But I knew with this book, the art needed to take a different direction. I decided early on that there would be no borders for the panels of the word balloons. I wanted this to feel like a memory as much as I wanted the reader to immediately feel present with the protagonist. While I used digital tools to piece together the final art, the majority of it was crafted with good old-fashioned tangible tools. The sketching was done with pencil on paper, which was then scanned in and adjusted to accommodate text. Those digital files were printed out and placed on a light board, where I created the final line work by applying ink to Bristol board with a brush pen. That line work was scanned in and I made minor digital edits. Those digital files were printed out and it was back to the light box, where another piece of Bristol board was placed over the line work, and I applied washes of ink with various brushes. Those washes were then scanned in, and in Photoshop I carved out blocks of white, using a digital brush that replicated a Conté crayon. After, I layered in washes of orange with a digital brush that replicated watercolors.

As I created the artwork, I kept remembering something that my art instructor, mentor, and dear friend, Mark Lynch, told me when I was a teenager: Celebrate your own style. Had he not told me that and introduced me to so many different kinds of comic arts, I don't think I ever would have had the courage to dive in to approaching the artwork as I did for this graphic memoir.

You'll find artifacts from my past and my family's past throughout this book. With the exception of Joe's sketch made during WWII and the Rotten Ralph drawing, everything is historically authentic. My grandfather always encouraged me to hold on to artwork and mementos that were important to me. Because of that, I have a treasure trove of artworks from throughout my childhood. Whenever you see the character Jarrett drawing, it is actual artwork that I made at his age. While my mother was incarcerated, she sent me a lot of letters and a lot of drawings. Her drawings inspired me and encouraged me to do something productive with the same gifts I had been given. I'm proud to share my mother's drawings with you in this book. My grandfather was a very talented artist too, but the only drawing of his that I knew existed was in his WWII journal. That journal went missing while I wrote this book. Although I wasn't able to track down the journal through family members, I wanted to acknowledge my grandfather's artistic talents, so I re-created his drawing as best I could and photoshopped in his initials.

You'll also notice the pineapple wallpaper. My grandmother was obsessed with pineapples—I mean, who else would choose pineapple wallpaper? When it came time to sell our childhood home, the family worked on emptying it out. I came across an unused roll of that pineapple wallpaper and saved it. I'm an artist — you just never know how you might use found materials for a piece. Well, more than a decade later, I was able to use it in this book, modifying it by painting over it and collaging it into the art of the book.

Creating the art for this book has been the most profound artistic endeavor I have yet to undertake and it has truly been a lifetime in the making.

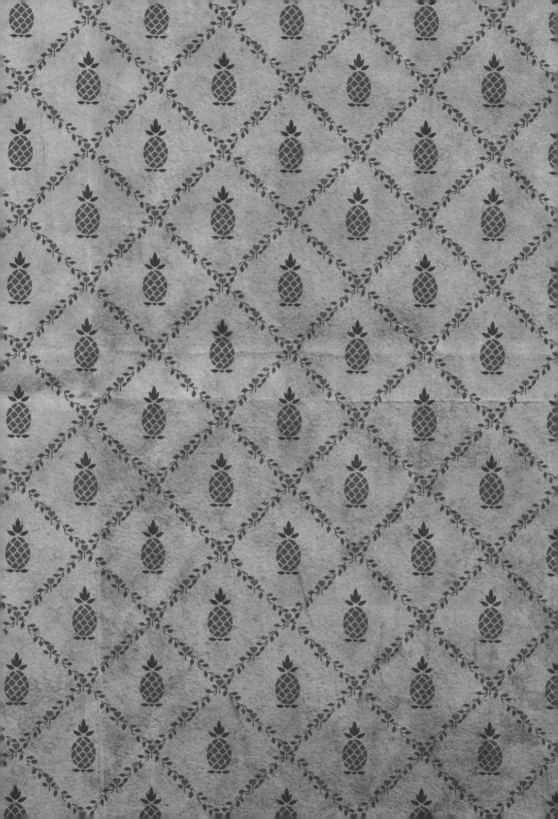

ACKNOWLEDGMENTS

In October of 2012, I stood before the TED cameras and shared a part of my truth with the world. I talked about my mother's addiction to heroin, shared my lifelong passion for drawing, and introduced the grandparents who raised me and ordered their drinks stiff. Once that video hit the Internet, I received a global response from strangers who saw themselves in my story. It empowered me. Before delivering that eighteen-minute speech, I had been working on a graphic memoir, but I'd been holding back. The response to what I said gave me the strength to tell my story with a much more brutal honesty.

But how did I get the courage to tell my story in front of the TED cameras in the first place? My wife, Gina. After I accepted the invitation (with only four hours' notice!), I paced the floor of our kitchen, wondering aloud what to talk about.

"Isn't it obvious?" Gina asked. "Tell them about your upbringing."

I shot out a few ideas. "I'll say, 'My mother was a drug addict.'"

Gina cut me off. "No. Be honest. Your mother was a heroin addict. Say that."

Gina encouraged me to share my story that day, just as she has encouraged my spirit since the day we met. She has supported me, lifted me up, and given me honest opinions whenever I really need them—whether I'm ready to hear them or not. Writing and illustrating this book forced me to revisit some very dark places, and creating the artwork took countless hours that took me away from our family on many nights and weekend days. Throughout the process, Gina has been very patient and remarkably strong.

I could not have revisited the difficult moments without my friend and editor, David Levithan. A true friend can pick up meanings behind retorts, and a great editor can take a story and move things around to make it infinitely better. David is both of these things and more. I am eternally grateful to have him help me craft stories and to swap mix CDs with.

I am so lucky to have Phil Falco working on the design and art direction of this book. He is an immense talent. (Those chapter openers? Dang.) Thank you, too, to the entire team at Scholastic who have taken this journey with me to get this story out into the world—Lauren Donovan, Lizette Serrano, Tracy van Straaten, Rachel Feld, and the entire sales, marketing, and production teams.

Thank you to my early readers—Angela, Jeannie, Noam, Raina, Cece, and Tom—whose encouragement lifted me up at a crucial time in the writing process.

To Holly, Lynn, and Steve—thank you for reading through the early script and letting me know that my memories were in line with what actually happened. You lived through this, too, and I'm lucky to have had you looking over me as I grew up. I hope this book helps bring even more Joe and Shirl back into your life. I know that you, too, think about them every single day.

Thank you to my sister and brother literally from another mother, Rich and Maura, for reading the early draft for this book. It's something close to a miracle that I found you, and I'm grateful to have you in my life.

Jarrett J. Krosoczka is a *New York Times* bestselling author and illustrator who has published dozens of books, including the Lunch Lady graphic novels, the Platypus Police Squad middle grade novels, and arcs in the Star Wars: Jedi Academy series. He was first published when he was only twenty-three years old. Jarrett's TED Talk about his childhood has been viewed over a million times and can be found on his website at www.studiojjk.com.

Jarrett was designated as a Distinguished Alumni of the Worcester Public Schools, which was acknowledged with a key to the city, and he has been inducted into the Holy Name Central Catholic High School Hall of Fame, where his mural *Light Switch Napoleon* is still displayed.

Jarrett lives in western Massachusetts with his wife, children, and two pugs.

A huge thank-you to Sam Hoffman, my art assistant, who kept everything moving along in the studio, and whose scanning, organizing, and file prep helped me get the art for this book delivered.

Thank you to the librarians at the Worcester Public Library and the Worcester Historical Museum who helped with research, and thank you to Sandy Hanlan, who provided some great photos of life growing up in the old neighborhood.

Thank you to my literary agent, Rebecca Sherman. On our first meeting a dozen or so years ago, she asked me what my dream book was. I described the book that you are holding in your hands. Rebecca has worked tirelessly for me as I worked on book after book. She's also good for swapping theater puns.

Most of all, thank you to my family. Gina, Zoe, Lucia, and Xavier, I love you more.